The Bright Side of Failure

The silent journey where your failures become the greatest motivation for your success!

By Karishma Archana

All quotes featured in this book are credited to their respective owners.

Email: contacttkarishma@gmail.com

Introduction to the Book

Failure - The most overrated phase of life.

People often say that success has different definitions for everyone, but I think, the same is true for failure. Each person's experience with failure is different, but we rarely acknowledge this fact.

Despite being an inevitable part of life, many struggle to accept and deal with it. You can't learn without failing, yet people often falter in the face of failure.

This book won't promise you success in all your endeavors, but it will help you change how you perceive the loss.

We need to change how we see failure, especially for today's teenagers. This book is a small effort to help change their way of thinking.

It's important to understand how your perspective during this key learning stage can change your whole life.

Failure is not the end, but a beginning; an indicator of progress.

You might have encountered the concepts in this book before, but here you will see them from a new perspective.

What matters most is how you see the events.

So, let's get on the journey where your failures become the greatest motivation for your success.

____

Table of Content

If you are failing,
you are not ALONE!

This book is a ray of hope for those who are tired of their setbacks and looking for just one chance to make a strong comeback!

This is a reminder to them:

"The race is not finished yet, because you are yet to win!"

Life is too short to be stuck on one loss.

*Accept it, learn from it,
and keep moving forward.*

Chapter 1

The Art of Learning from Mistakes!

I read somewhere,

"If you fail, never give up. Because
***FAIL** means "**First Attempt in Learning**."*
The End is not the end.
***END** Means "**Effort Never Dies**.*
*And, if you get **NO** as an answer,*
*it means, **Next Opportunity**."*

Failure is treated as a disease or let me say a pandemic in our society, whose medicine is yet to be discovered.

Imagine, you fell into the well. No one is around to help you. You are howling as loud as you can, but there is no one to help you, but only you and yourself. What would you do?

Okay, as a human nature, you are scared, no doubt. But, would you not even try to come out of it? Will you be sitting quietly waiting for someone to come and save you?

It's clearly, a big NO. Right?

When it comes to protecting your life, you do whatever you can to make sure you are safe. Isn't it?

Failure is like that deep and dark well holding you back in the same place. You don't understand, what should I do? How to deal with it? Who should I reach out to? How do I come out of this situation? How do I handle that failure tag? And what not making a way clear for overthinking.

The biggest reason behind this situation is that we are not taught to face failure. What we know is;

"Once a failure, always is a failure."

However, we are supposed to win and only win the race, no matter at what cost.

Failure is never seen as a learning phase by the so-called educated and competitive society.

All they know is;

Failure means **The End.**

Failure!

The scariest word, no one wants to listen, nor does anyone want to be called a *Failure*.

But the question is; when every successful person has a failure story, then why does failure get too much hate by the people? And why it is a taboo in our society? And not a learning?

Failure never comes alone.

It will always knock on your door with his two partners. One is an *experience*, and the other is a *success*, and both of these things pay you for your efforts.

A quote I remember,

*"Success comes from experience,
and experience comes from a bad experience."*

Experience is the best teacher. No one can teach you what an experience teaches you.

Every failure teaches you one lesson. Those who understand it gets to see success, and those who stays with that one loss, can never rise.

It's nothing but an art to learn from your mistakes and not repeating those mistakes again instead of blaming it.

Success means;
FALL, RISE, AND KEEP MOVING.

Let me say, you are walking on a road, and your leg hits a stone that you didn't see.

While coming back on the same route, you will recognize that you had an injury here and will be more conscious while walking through the path. This is what an experience does.

Now, you can walk through the same path with awareness and guide others to walk carefully, preventing them from suffering the same injury you recently sustained.

When you fail, you never count it as an experience. And, here, you start a real journey towards being an actual failure.

You might have played with an ant in your childhood, putting an obstacle in its way to stop it. But did it stop?

No, right?

It never stops. It keeps walking until it reaches its destination.

No matter how many times you tried to stop it, you eventually stopped bothering it and let it go, but it never stopped trying to reach its destination.

Success is like that ant, and failure is like that obstacle. No matter how many times you face failure, you will succeed if you maintain consistency in your efforts.

Never underestimate the power of
CONSISTENCY.

Know your goal, and keep working on it again and again and again until success hugs you.

Do you remember who invented the electric bulb?

Thomas Elva Edison!

Everyone is aware of the bulb's evolution. It was a long-long journey with no known destination.

Thomas Edison didn't know when and where he would be successful. But he knew his GOAL.

Walking on a path where you don't know how long you need to walk to win presents a real challenge. And trust me, it's not easy at all.

He only knew what he wanted to achieve, regardless of cost, time, and effort. But, how? The answer was not known.

When he finally succeeded, he said,

*"I have not failed.
I have just found 10,000 ways that won't work."*

Can you imagine his dedication and consistency in work?

Until you are ready to accept failure, you can't get success, though.

What you can learn from this incident is a positive way of looking at the situation. Having a vision where you can see the loss as a learning is very important.

I met many people who made a plan and walked through it to make it successful. Which is so obvious.

At the same time, you can't ignore the probability of getting things *not as planned*. It's always a 50-50 share. Isn't it?

If things don't go as planned, things are destroyed for people. Eventually, they don't have a plan B to tackle the situation.

Like, really???

Can you remember, when you were learning how to ride a bicycle, didn't you fall? Of course, yes. But, did you just give up on learning, or start again? And after so many falls, you learned to cycle.

YES, YOU DID IT!

And, you should be proud of yourself for this learning! It teaches a very important lesson.

Chapter 2

A Tale of
Biggest Failure!

Dr. A. P. J. Abdul Kalam believes that the youth is a very powerful Army and the future of our country. But, unfortunately, this youth, today, is failed in facing failure.

Do you know that the *Missile Man of India* himself is a failure? Yes, It's true!

Let me share an incident about Dr. Abdul Kalam with you that he shared in a speech.

While speaking, he shared his failure story, when he failed at launching a satellite at Sriharikota as a mission director.

So, the incident happened in 1979, at the time of the SLV-3 launch.

It would be one of the big missions, as thousands of people worked on it for nearly ten years. The mission aimed at putting the satellite into orbit.

The mission was under the supervision of Dr. Abdul Kalam. All the arrangements were made.

No doubt, any mission or, as of here, let's say, satellite launching requires a lot of effort, a very long time, and heavy funding.

Just before a few seconds to go, the team detects some technical error on the computer screen. They found a glitch with some oil leakage in the control system.

However, after doing some quick calculations, Dr. Kalam and the team concluded that the satellite had enough fuel to launch even after the leakage.

Still, the final decision to go ahead with the mission or to abort it was entirely Dr. Kalam's call.

If Dr. Kalam launched the satellite and the mission failed, the millions of bucks and years of effort would be in vain.

And, if he cancels the task, the ISRO will lose the government's trust and the country's people's faith. So, the decision was difficult.

And, he finally said, "*YES.*"

After the decision was made, the satellite was launched. It was a 4 stage satellite.

In the first stage, the work was as expected. But, as the satellite entered the second stage, it began to spin madly and fell into the Bay of Bengal.

It was a massive loss for Dr. Kalam and, of course, the country. It was the major *'FAILURE'* Dr. Kalam experienced.

After this failure, the team needed to address a press conference. The day came, and a lot of media persons were ready to confront the group. Dr. Kalam was so scared and nervous.

At that time, Prof. Satish Dhawan, the chairman of ISRO, moved toward Dr. Kalam and said, "*let's face the press conference.*" Media personnel confronted the team badly for wasting millions of bucks.

To all their questions, Prof. Dhawan answered,

"We have failed today, I take the blame, and I applaud my team for putting in all their efforts; we will come back very soon with our next project, and we will succeed in this."

The ISRO team, on July 18, 1980, re-entered with the second version of SLV-3. It carried Rohini satellite -1. The satellite had a Magnetometer, a Digital Sun Sensor, and a temperature sensor.

This time, the mission was successful. And the satellite was rested in orbit.

One more thing that Dr. Kalam shared. He said, *"When after the mission-2 success, the press conference was scheduled again. And this time, Prof. Dhawan came to me and asked me to go alone in front of the media personnel."*

He continued,

"The leader was present during our failure times. Also, he took all the blame. But, he asked us to face media personnel alone when we succeed."

You can't even imagine how huge the loss was.

This incident teaches many things to everyone who gets disappointed due to the failure.

Indeed, you will feel bad; you may lose hope for instance. But, if you keep holding yourself back to the point where you fail, you lose there.

If Dr. Kalam and his team had been cursing their mistake and stuck in the past failure, was the success possible?

NO.

Nothing can work until you leave your mistakes in the past, learn from them, and take another step toward your goal.

"You are not a failure until you say it to yourself."

I believe failure doesn't exist at all. Or it does in your mind…

Just like, while driving, you see speed breakers that are meant to have you; the loss is the speed breaker that builds you.

It makes you see within yourself and find out the best in you.

Failure is a comma (,), and the race is yet to be finished. You have to walk until you find a full stop(.) which makes your journey complete.

And for that, you have to keep learning.

When you stop learning and exploring new things, you start pushing the breaks to your wheel, and you won't be able to walk for a long run.

Remember, learning should be consistent.

Once you find your *full stop* (.) doesn't mean you have to stop.

Rather, take the inspiration from your own achievement, and say,

"if I can do this, I can achieve anything in the world."

Make your own achievements your biggest inspiration.

Believe in yourself, and keep working on your own every single day to shine brighter.

There is a famous saying –

"Success hugs you in private, while failure slaps you in public."

As much as this is true, no one tries to understand the reason for your failure and the struggle you have to get your winning moment. And unfortunately, you failed.

Everyone will try to pull your leg and tie you with your loss. But, you have to be strong enough to break the rope and run again.

Once, I heard about a person who cleared his IAS exam in his very first chance. He said,

"No one knows what I did. How do I struggle? What did I sacrifice? But when I succeeded in my goal, people said, 'Tumara luck acha hai' (your luck is your side), that you clear the world's most challenging exam in one attempt."

Once you get success, people won't care how challenging your journey was. They know how to praise you when you succeed and blame you when you are failed.

These things have made failure a social stigma rather than a way to learn and sharpen your traits. And, this is the big reason why failure seems too scary.

Remember, dealing with failure also means learning the act of acceptance: *"Kuch to log kahenge, logoka kam hai kehna (People will always have something to say; it's just what they do)."*

You don't need to be vocal about each comment people make on you. Just listen, ignore, and get back to your work. Believe me, you have to learn to ignore people and their judgments on you.

Accept the fact first that you failed, and people will judge you on that. But don't let this fact defeat you. Acceptance makes you stronger (if taken positively).

Accept the reality and know your capabilities. Have faith in yourself, and keep working on your aim.

The journey from failure to success is indeed tough, but not impossible.

Let your victory make noise, not your words.

Chapter 3

Fear of Failure (Atychiphobia)

Albert Einstein once said –

*"A person who never made a mistake
never tried anything new."*

You have a phobia. It's not about trying anything new, but you are scared to fail and then see people judging you.

So, even when you try something new and unique, people anyway comment on you, pass their judgment, and try to demotivate you unless and until they see you doing good. They want to take credit for your success and absolve themselves in your failure.

Fear of failure, also called, Atychiphobia, makes you not try something new at all, and you quit the decision of even attempting it.

This is a Greek-originated word; "atyches" means "unfortunate," and "phobia" stands for fear.

In this situation, the person who is experiencing the intense fear of failure avoids situations where they see the potential to fail. It's more of a fear of shame after losing.

It causes you to do nothing. You don't even try to think of the other side of trying, which is getting success.

Fear of failure doesn't allow you to see the opportunities that are in front of you to succeed.

But, what factors trigger this fear?

Before knowing the causes, you need to understand what failure is.

The definition of failure can be different for everyone, as everyone has different goals, benchmarks, beliefs, and values.

However, a failure can be a bunch of experiences for someone, while for others, it can be the end of their journey.

Fear of failure can come from different reasons, such as a prior bad experience that left you with mixed emotions, including shame or the impact of being bullied.

Let me say if you were all set to rock the stage with your amazing speech in front of a huge crowd. You were too confident but you ended up getting frozen on the stage and not saying a single word. Well, that was me when I was in school.

Anyway, it was my first time delivering a speech on a stage. I was so excited at the same time very nervous. Yet, that one experience is still present in my subconscious mind and it led me to a stage-fear.

This was the terrifying experience I had many years ago. And, I could never amplify that emotion. Thus, I started having fear to try something new, because, in that situation I pushed my limits and tried to do something new, and I failed.

But I never stopped trying new things. That was one bad experience, but I was able to move past it to some degree.

The other case could be an unsupportive and humiliating behavior of the parents that stimulates negative emotions in a kid. And it stays with them till their adulthood.

Comparison among two kids is like comparing the abilities of water and fire.

Two people can never be the same, nor their capacities, emotions, thoughts, or intelligence.

Such experience induces fear in kids of falling, and failing, and they start doubting themselves.

The experience can cause lower self-esteem and lower self-confidence.

You want to try only those things you know you are an expert with and can achieve perfection.

How you look at failure is entirely your call. It is up to you whether you see failure as the *'end of your world'* or an *"incredible experience."*

Failure can't stop you until you allow it to do this.

Every single time you get failed, you need to try to find what you can learn from it. What mistakes did you make that resulted in this failure? And how can you make it right?

Mistakes are meant to be a teacher.

Failures are not as bad as you think. Instead, you can see successful people getting failed. Yet, they created history.

Warren Buffet, one of the world's wealthiest and most successful businessmen, was rejected by Harvard University.

Walt Disney was fired from the *Kansas City Star* because the editor believed he lacked imagination and creative ideas.

J. K. Rowling had faced 12 times rejection of her Harry Potter series before Bloomsbury accepted it.

Not just these, but every successful person has a story of failure.

Maybe, after facing repeated failures, they lost hope, but they continued to try until they achieved success.

The very live example can be Albert Einstein. He says,

"I have tried 99 times
 and have failed,
but on the 100th time
came success."

I know, when you constantly fail, it becomes so challenging to keep consistency with patience.

But remember, great work doesn't come out until you take risks.

Failure teaches you unexpected aspects about yourself. You start finding values that motivate you to get your win.

When you face loss constantly, you begin to know about your strengths; you start thinking of all those ways to achieve your goal. Or maybe, some other ways to achieve things that you dreamed of.

When you try something, there is an equal chance that you will fail. So, be prepared for it. And remember,

"When one door closes, ten others open."

What you need to do is look for those open doors.

Having the *self-confidence* to get success is an important part of a positive attitude. But you can't ignore those chances of getting failed.

So, if you are ready to accept whatever comes in the end, makes you stronger enough to face failure. Rather, you should make plans accordingly.

Maybe you can have a *Plan B*, so that, if you fail you don't find yourself as a loser. This can be the most hopeful way to deal with the fear of failure.

When you are working on plan A (which is your ultimate goal), keep plan B in mind. Who knows? Maybe that Plan B is your way to success.

What you have is, trying and taking risks for plan A. But, plan B is that stepney you always have in your car in case any of the working wheels fail.

And remember, having another plan is not a bad decision. It shows your strength and presents you as a warrior.

*"Failure is not the
opposite of success.
But, it is the part of success."*

Success doesn't come without failing you.

If you think you only want to succeed without getting failed, it won't happen *(If you win on your first try, celebrate it).*

You need to accept your failure as a *TREAT*.

Failure doesn't stay with you for a lifetime. See it as a bonus. And bonuses are always enjoyable. Right?

You must learn to accept failure when it comes your way. But, don't choose to quit *TRYING*.

When you stop trying, you fail there and not at the point when you lose something.

You are not a failure until you accept yourself as a failure.

Chapter 4

You Fail. You Win!

The Perception

Jack Canfield says—

*"Don't worry about the mistakes;
worry about the chance you miss when
you don't even try."*

Your perception looking at failure makes you a winner or a loser.

Remember, failure is not the end. But it is the start of your journey towards your goal. And anyway, you are failing because you are not trying to do something towards your goal.

Today, every successful person is not successful because they were such a bright student, they had planned their journey, and they never failed or they had some supernatural powers. But they turned their failure into victory.

For them, failure was not a loss, but it was the opportunity they grabbed that spun their life.

Everyone wants victory. But when you lose, you need to see it as a chance on your table to make you a better version of yourself.

Ask yourself,

"If I fail, do I have a backup plan to handle it?"

You might have a list of what you will do when you achieve your goal. But you need to understand that failure is not an option and, no one chooses it. But, still, sometimes you get it served on your table.

And, you have to face it.

If you have a question paper in front of you, you only can write the answers to those questions. You can't change the questions or the result, which is supposed to decide your future.

To explain this, Robert Kiyosaki says,

*"Successful people
don't fear failure,
but understand that it's necessary to
learn and grow from."*

I'm sure many of you follow the cricket matches. But, do you know what it teaches beyond the game?

In every match, one team wins against the other. But this doesn't mean that the losing team was a loser, and they will never play any game again.

Instead, in the next match, the losing team gets another chance and wins. No team seats in the back chair, regretting their defeat with the first team.

Talking about the players, if one player gets out on the first ball, it doesn't mean he is a bad player. He doesn't sit back and stays on that one mistake for the rest of his life.

Rather than focusing on the failure, he began to identify his mistake and correct it.

In the next game, he enters the field with full enthusiasm and claims victory.

When a player gets out on the first ball, people may criticize him with harsh comments. But does he pay attention to them, or does he double his practice and prove himself in the next match? He chose the second option.

And that's why he is where he is now.

<u>**The Right Time**</u>

There is one more thing that is very helpful in your journey from failure to success; i.e., *THE TIME.*

A quote says;

*"If you won't respect the TIME,
the TIME won't respect you."*

Success has no set criteria for achieving it, except for the simple rule of never giving up.

No matter your gender, age, education, or religion, success is something everyone can achieve. But, the one, who respects time, is the one who achieves success.

You should never wait for the right time. When you start working on your goal, it is the right time.

The so-called right time never comes. It is you who turns the time into *"The Right Time."*

You have to be careful about spending your time. If you have decided to achieve something, put in all your efforts. Also, remember, if one method isn't working, try changing your approach.

Don't let your goal fade; hit the ball and send it out of the stadium.

The Right Decision

One more thing that holds you back is the *Decisions* you make.

No one is perfect, thus their decisions. And your choices have an important role in your journey.

Let me share an experience of mine.

I was unsure of what to do after completing my HSC exam. Which field would be the best fit for me? What should I do next?

Not everyone has a pre-decided plan. I was just as clueless. And as you know, this is a crucial stage in a student's life, one on which their entire future depends.

Okay, I won't say that wrong decisions can't be corrected. But sometimes it takes years to correct them.

Meanwhile, it's a war between your existence, reality, and your mental peace. Trust me, for those who are hungry for success, this means a lot.

After choosing one of the suggested fields, I finished my graduation.

Choosing the right course of study is like being on a ventilator, giving you the necessary support to live until you finish it. And, in my case, the decision was wrong.

Even after having a professional degree, I was not feeling enthusiastic about working in the domain. And, those, who are sailing in the same boat as me, only can understand how critical this situation can be.

You start questioning your existence. Your mental and social battle begins here. You anyway doubt yourself and people start questioning about your job, work, and so on.

Being from a humble background, this decision would have a major effect on my future.

It means I wasted my last few years, which are never going to come back. I just wanted to go back to the time when I made that decision and correct it.

In short, I failed to build the foundation of my career. And this thought was killing me every single minute.

I remember when I lost my first job because the operation of the company was shut down, I started looking back at my degrees, finding them useless. I was in a new city.

One night, around 2 AM, I came out of my room and sat on the stairs. My overthinking wouldn't let me sleep.

Though that was my very first job, for me, it was a really big deal. It took me a long time to realize that losing this job wasn't the end of everything. I can still achieve anything I want.

I was raised by a single parent, and all I wanted was to get a job as soon as possible to help her. Every middle-class person feels this, right?

I took out all my degree certificates and exam results and stared at them, feeling like a loser. They all seemed like nothing more than pieces of paper with zero value in my life.

For three months, I didn't tell my family that I had lost my job. I was trying to find another one, but all my attempts had failed. Going for interviews and returning home without any hope was not easy.

I remember those sleepless nights, crying and worrying about the future, confronting myself for that one wrong decision. I was all alone away from my family.

I had only two options: accept the wrong decision I made and try to fit into an environment that wasn't right for me, or find a path that would lead me to the new world.

I choose the second option. And today, you are reading my Book.

Isn't it an achievement for me?

Remember, your decisions don't always have to be always correct. But when you make a decision, you must make sure it's the right one.

Decisions go wrong in life, and life goes wrong. But, the only thing that can take you out of this, is the trust you have in yourself.

Have faith in yourself. If you can't trust and respect yourself, you can't expect others to do the same.

It's life, which is more complicated than the jigsaw puzzle. Before you begin solving one problem in front of you, it may present you with a new one.

And this is how it began to get more complicated.

What your wrong decision does is hold you to the moment you made it, making you blame yourself.

You can't move on from past choices, and this becomes the biggest obstacle between you and your success.

You need to understand that failure is actually a victory. Because

"The road to success and the road to failure are almost the same."

To understand this, you need to have a positive attitude.

A positive attitude is itself a strength that helps you all the way long.

Unless you try to find something good in the worst situation, you will stop getting achievements.

The difficult situations are like exams; you have to pass them. If you approach these challenges with optimism, you will learn valuable lessons in life.

You need to change the way you look at the tough times, and you will realize that they make you stronger.

Successful people know this formula. So, you won't find any of the successful people complaining about their tough times.

Instead, they are always grateful for their difficult situations. They are who they are today because of those challenging times.

Chapter 5

Failure is Your Identity....?

F. Dean Hackett says –

"Failure is an event, not an identity."

Don't let failure be your identity.

You make mistakes, learn from them, fix them, and try again. Failure helps you learn and grow towards success.

As F. Dean Hackett says, failure is an event. And, no event lasts for a lifetime. There comes a point at which the event must end.

Failure has an expiry date, and it's up to you to decide what that date will be.

Our life revolves around the events of failure.

When you give your best, put your heart into something, and it fails, it feels like everything you hoped for just disappears.

Failure can turn your life upside down, making you forget that it's actually a ladder leading you to your goals.

All the successful people were failures. But, no one knows them for their losses but for their victories. Neither are they afraid to share their failure stories.

They know that the failure they faced was the reason they are in their current position.

Failure doesn't make you weak, but it strengthens you in all ways.

One of the guys I know started his business 4 years ago. Unfortunately, it didn't succeed, and he had to shut the operation despite all the financial and mental effort he invested.

When you stake everything into something and then fail, it's not easy to handle. I understand. But it's important to face the reality.

He said,

"It wasn't a failure on my part. I learned from the experience what not to do in the future. While this business didn't succeed, I'm not defeated. I'm going to restart it, knowing what won't work, and I won't make those mistakes again."

Isn't it the perfect example of a positive attitude?

If that guy failed, this doesn't mean he lacked in his efforts. I saw him working so hard day and night for his business. Still, things didn't work out for him. As a result, he had to face failure.

But, one thing that makes him different from others is his perception looking at his loss.

He is as enthusiastic as ever, not blaming any external factors. He has taken this loss as a lesson and is ready to start again. And, I'm sure, he will definitely be successful, because of his positive attitude.

You all need to learn that attempting something is in your hands. But, the outcome is beyond your control.

Yes, your efforts, commitment, and hard work are within your control. But, expecting only success can break you completely.

Because, in such cases, your mind is only ready to accept success, and it refuses to accept and face failure. And, you start getting lost in all ways.

You make one more mistake: comparing your journey with others.

"Don't compare your life
with others.
There's no comparison between the
sun and the moon.
They shine when it's their time."

If someone is getting success quickly, it doesn't mean you are bad at something, undeserving, good for nothing, or your luck is terrible.

Remember, in your journey to be successful, your luck helps you only 1%. The rest of the 99% is your efforts.

You can't rely on the luck and wait for it to shine for you. It won't happen ever.

If you compare your journey with others, you are insulting your capabilities. There's nothing the same in between you two.

Their struggle was different from yours. Their dream, their efforts, and the way to success are different, and you can't follow their path.

Success feels incomplete without a story of failure. Everyone faces failure, rejection, and disappointment. But, when they don't give up, they shine.

This doesn't mean you can't succeed without failing along the way. Remember the 1:99 ratios- when both luck and success come together, they create 100% of what you need to achieve your goals.

There is no rule that you must fail first to succeed. But, the true joy of success comes only after experiencing failure, which was of course not your plan, yet you get it.

Correct?

I remember one of the readings,

"Don't read success stories;
you will only get a message.
Read failure stories; you will get some
ideas to get success."

This quote suggests you to follow the failure stories of successful people.

In return, it will offer you two rewards; first, you will realize that no one had the same journey, and second, you will find dozens of solutions to your problems.

Although their approach to dealing with a problem may not work for you. But you might find the solution you have been searching for.

Choose your path. No one cares how challenging your journey was, how hard the sacrifices were, or what you lost along the way.

Although people judge you based on your failures, the same ones will praise you when you succeed.

Failure and success may seem like opposites, with failure often seen as the point where victory ends and success as the result of hard work. But you need to understand the relationship between the two.

Success never comes without its share of losses. When failure becomes frequent, you are actually on the road to growth (of course with the right approach).

The key is to learn from every setback, rather than blaming the situations around you.

What you have to learn is, when you get failed, don't be scared of it.

After years of working towards your goal, it's natural to feel sad when you fail. You may feel like crying out loud, letting the universe feel your pain.

Let your emotions flow.

Remember, never suppress how you feel; express them.

When you try to hold these emotions, it works as poison for your mind. They start affecting you and leading you to anxiety and stress. And, you have to protect yourself from getting lost.

It is unknowingly the first step towards making your identity as a failure.

Step out of your comfort zone.

It's the biggest barrier between you and your success. Always believe in yourself, and no one will be able to stop you from achieving your goals.

Chapter 6

Don't Succeed at Failing!

Ralph Waldo Emerson said-

*"The only person you are
destined to become,
is the person you decide to be."*

What do you think destiny really is?

Is destiny something you create, something you live through, or something predetermined?

Think about a time when something bad happened-did you blame destiny? And when you succeeded, did you credit destiny or your hard work?

Many believe destiny is written by God or in the lines of their hands.

But is it really true?

The truth is, *you* write your own destiny.

If it were prewritten, those who failed multiple times would never succeed. But they do-because destiny isn't fate, it's the result of your actions.

It is often said that,

"Life is a book, whose first and the last page are written with birth and death, respectively.
The rest of the middle pages are blank that you are supposed to fill out."

I believe those blank pages are your destiny, that you are writing and not pre-written.

Of course, the first and last pages are already written with birth and death. But the entire story in between is yours to write.

It's you who write every chapter in the book each day, each minute, and every second of your life. Your thoughts, feelings, and actions are the chapters you write in the story of your life.

Most of the pages of your book are written with lessons on failure and learning.

Think about your life, from childhood to adulthood. Every experience, whether good or bad, has contributed to the person you are today.

Everyone has faced failure at some point. Still, no one admits it. But only those who accept their setbacks can rise and reach success.

Can you honestly raise your hand and say, *"I have never failed in my life?"*

If I had to answer this question, I would raise both of my hands.

Anyway!

If you say, I have not failed ever; you are lying to yourself. Or, you have never tried anything new so far.

From the moment you started learning to walk as a toddler, you have faced many failures.

You fell with each step, got up, walked again, and eventually learned to walk.

If you had sat there after your first fall, you would have never been able to walk.

I personally see failure as the steps that take me closer to my goal.

One more thing that helped me deal with my downfall was my perspective on failure. Every day, I fail, learn from it, and came back stronger.

The more you understand this, the more consciously you can deal with situations.

Your perspective on failure plays a key role in the entire journey of your life.

Another very important thing we often ignore is *ACCEPTANCE*.

Until you accept something, you can't deal with it. People stay in denial, but accepting the situation helps you move on.

Accept that you have failed an exam because you did not study well. Accept that you failed in your business because you lack somewhere with your plan and efforts.

There is a possibility that, you may not have lacked anything, but certain factors didn't align that leads failure. And realizing this is important.

If you stay in denial *"No, no. I didn't lack anything in my efforts. Everything I did was right, yet I still failed. I don't know how,"* then you will never be able to move on from that failure or achieve what you truly wanted.

Acknowledging this helps you learn and grow.

How many times will you blame external factors for your defeat? You can tell others a story about your failure, but you can't lie to yourself. And you exactly know the reason behind your loss.

Acceptance is the key, my friend.

Accept the fact, your mistakes, your ignorance towards the task, your laziness, and your procrastination.

Start working on your goal right now.

It's entirely up to you, either you can face the reality and make things right, or you can choose to stay in the world of denial.

Faith and hard work build your destiny. Your beliefs will decide your actions.

If you think your path is already set, you won't try to change it. But if you believe in your ability to change your future, you will put in the hard work to make it amazing and motivate others along the way.

Failure is a tough part of the journey, but it's necessary. Without failure, success wouldn't be possible.

Remember, a single failure or multiple failures don't define you as a loser.

Failure is simply another step toward success. All you need is to change your perspective on loss.

Don't let failure define who you are. It's just a moment in time that doesn't dictate your future success.

Failure is the end of one chapter, but the start of a new journey.

So, keep going, and eventually, you will succeed.

And listen,

I AM SO PROUD OF YOU
*for every effort, every step, and every little win
along the way!*

Keep going!

No wonder!

**You are a magician to turn your
failure into your success.**
Have faith in yourself,
and you will achieve everything you want.

www.ingramcontent.com/pod-product-compliance
Lightning Source LLC
Chambersburg PA
CBHW031319130726
47988CB00007B/2899